THE FIRSTS

FASCINATING FACTS

David Armentrout

The Rourke Press, Inc.
o Beach, Florida 32964

PHOTO CREDITS
© Evelyn Bloom: Right Cover, pg. 8; © Cincinnati Historical
Society: pg. 21; © Corel Corporation: pg. 10; © Kim Karpeles: pg.
17; © NASA: Left Cover, pg. 18; © James P. Rowan: pgs. 7, 12;
© Smithsonian Institution Museum of American History: pg. 15;
© Thomson Consumer Electronics: pg. 13; © Ryan Williams/Int'l
Stock: pg. 4; © Marty Youngmann: Title page

Library of Congress Cataloging-in-Publication Data

Armentrout, David, 1962–
   The firsts / by David Armentrout.
     p. cm. — (Fascinating facts)
   ISBN 1-57103-128-6
   1. Curiosities and wonders—Juvenile literature. 2. World
records—Juvenile literature.
I. Title II. Series: Armentrout, David, 1962- Fascinating facts.
AG243.A6 1996
031.02—dc20   96–23843
                                                    CIP
                                                    AC

Printed in the USA

TABLE OF CONTENTS

OLYMPIC GAMES

Did you know that the first **Olympic games** (o LIM pik) (GAYMZ) were held more than 2,000 years ago in ancient Greece?

Today's games begin when a torch is lighted. The torch is carried into the arena by the Greek team in honor of those first games.

The ancient games included performances of music and theater, as well as athletic events. The Olympic games now include a wide range of sporting events, such as snow skiing, ice hockey, swimming, and track and field.

BATTLE OF THE AMERICAN REVOLUTION

The American Revolution began because American colonies wanted freedom from British control.

British "Red Coats" and American colonists began fighting in April, 1775, in Lexington and Concord, Massachusetts. The first major battle, called the Battle of Bunker Hill, occurred in June that same year.

Independence (IN di PEN dens) from Great Britain was declared on July 4, 1776, although fighting continued until 1783. The United States celebrates Independence Day every year on the Fourth of July.

These men are dressed like the British Army in a Revolutionary War re-enactment

HOT AIR BALLOON

Joseph and Jacques Montgolfier sent the first hot air balloon into the sky in 1783. Hot air inside the balloon caused the balloon to rise. Then the air cooled and the balloon sunk to the ground.

Modern balloonists carry a small propane burner that heats air and keeps the balloon aloft. From Great Britain, Richard Branson and Per Lindstrand made the first hot air balloon flight across the Atlantic Ocean. Their journey of 3,075 miles took 31 hours and 41 minutes.

PRESIDENT

George Washington is called "Father of His Country" because of all his hard work for the first government of the United States.

George Washington was a leader in the battles of the American Revolution from 1775 to 1781. Washington also led a convention meeting of leaders, that adopted the U.S. **Constitution** (KAHN sti too shun).

By 1789, George Washington won the respect of many people who chose him to be the first President of the United States.

George Washington was the first President of the United States of America

The Bunker Hill Monument stands as a reminder of the first battle in the American Revolution

RCA's first color televisions were produced in an Indiana plant in 1954

PILOTS

Two brothers, Orville and Wilbur Wright, designed and built an engine and propeller for their glider.

They took the plane, named "Flyer 1," to a beach near Kitty Hawk, North Carolina on December 17, 1903. Orville Wright lay across the bottom wing of the plane. The small engine they had built powered the plane. Orville flew for 12 seconds while his brother Wilbur ran alongside.

The Wright Brothers were the first pilots of a motor-driven airplane.

Orville Wright takes his first flight while his brother Wilbur runs alongside

CAR

Henry Ford's motor company made the Model T Ford in 1908. The Model T was the first mass-produced car.

The first Model T cost $850. By 1914 Ford Motor Company made the Model T from a moving **assembly line** (uh SEM blee) (LYN). Assembly line work made the Model T cost less. By 1925 the price of the car had dropped to $290.

More than 15 million Model T's had been made by May 31, 1927, when the last one rolled off the assembly line.

The Model T Ford is a collector's item that is driven in antique car shows

MAN ON THE MOON

NASA (NAS uh) is the agency that launches every U.S. space flight. In 1961 NASA set up the Apollo program to take astronauts to the moon and back.

On July 20, 1969, the Apollo 11 lunar module landed on an area of the moon named Sea of Tranquility.

Neil Armstrong was the first man to set foot on the moon's surface. As he did, he spoke these words: "That's one small step for man, one giant leap for mankind."

This photograph of Astronaut Aldrin was taken by Astronaut Armstrong, the first man on the moon

BASEBALL TEAM

Who was the first baseball player? No one really knows. Legend has it that Abner Doubleday invented the game in Cooperstown, New York, in 1839.

Today, people of all ages all over the world play baseball. In North America, the best players are paid to play. Paid players are called professionals.

Professional baseball began in 1869 with the first team—the Cincinnati Red Stockings. The "Reds" traveled the country that year playing baseball before thousands of fans. They won 60 games without a loss!

The first professional baseball team was named Cincinnati Red Stockings

DEL   LEON VAN LO

THE
FIRST   NINE.

TELEVISION

The first television receiver was developed in the 1920's. By 1935 the U.S. had about 150 televisions. Today, the country has more than 100 million TV sets!

The RCA company displayed its first black-and-white TV's at the 1939 World's Fair. Very few shows were broadcast then.

Today, television offers many varied programs and has become an important source of news and entertainment.

Glossary

assembly line (uh SEM blee) (LYN) — machines and workers arranged so work passes from one step to the next until the product is put together

constitution (KAHN sti too shun) — a set of laws

independence (IN di PEN dens) — freedom from control

NASA (NAS uh) — National Aeronautics and Space Administration, an agency of the U.S. government

Olympic games (o LIM pik) (GAYMZ) — a series of modern athletic contests like ancient Greek festivals

INDEX